Reflections During a Monsoon Evening

Reflections During a Monsoon Evening

The Poems and Memories of a Vietnam Soldier

Michael Simay

Scythe Publications, Inc.

A Division of Winston-Derek Publishers Group, Inc.

PUBLISHED BY SCYTHE PUBLICATIONS, INC.
A Division of Winston-Derek Publishers Group, Inc.
Nashville, Tennessee 37205

Library of Congress Catalog Card No: 94-60944
ISBN: 1-55523-717-7

Printed in the United States of America

To God, who created us; to Christ, who redeemed us;
and to all of those who gave their lives
for our country and its Constitution.

Preface

Vietnam was the war of the infantryman. There were others, of course: the Special Forces soldiers (Green Berets), the cavalry troops, the artillery batteries, the helicopter pilots who, with guns blazing, came to help the infantry, and the "slicks," or transport choppers, HU-1's—we called them "Hueys"—that braved intense fire to take us into combat, or when wounded or dead, to take us out. And there were our angels, the combat nurses, whose cooling hands on our hot, mangled bodies were the last sensations we felt before we slipped into eternity. But no one lived, slept, feared, fought, or froze in the mud of the flooded paddies and mosquito infested swamps and jungles like the infantry. You could tell an infantryman by the way he wore his mud.

The infantryman saw the face of death more clearly because he saw it up close. He saw his friends die. He saw his enemies die. And hardest of all, he saw innocent children die. To the infantryman, *"inasmuch as ye have done it unto one of the least of these my brethren, ye have done it unto me,"* held special meaning.

All of these poems were written spontaneously between 1965 and 1973. I wrote them on note paper, "C" ration box tops, or whatever was handy. They are not works of art. In fact, I think they are poor as far as poems go because I am not a poet. I have not written a poem since then, nor will I write any more. These poems are not for, or against, war. They also never condemn the conscientious objector—*"blessed are the peacemakers."* These poems are against cowards, traitors, flag-burners, and those who take war lightly—whatever the reason.

I never intended to publish these poems, but the encouragement of my friends Karen Usher and Paul Stein changed my mind. Paul suggested that I also write about the events that prompted me to write each poem. Thus, after all the years, I read them and recalled the lonesome, bloody days and nights filled with strange emotions and strange things.

I took the photographs in this book while on combat operations with the 173rd Airborne Brigade. They represent an average day in the life of an American infantryman.

I have decided to donate the proceeds from this collection to charity. It is my hope that you too will give a few dollars to disabled veterans who may need wheelchairs, a place to eat and sleep, or who are down on their luck.

I Am

Sometimes, when day's end is near,
and the sun sends its last diffused light
from below the far horizon after the rain has ceased,
and only one drop seems with hesitation bound
from high above this earth toward this soggy ground
to cause one last ripple to be born and dissipate,
to die in this muddied pool, I watch
the reflection of that tree before me,
which has stood in this spot for who knows how many years,
along with my now darkened figure from the lack of light,
disappear in the ripple of a drop of rain,
coming from who knows where
and is forever swallowed up by night.

Ba Chuc, July 1966

A friend of mine died just a couple of days ago. He was shot through the head and stomach while trying to rescue a wounded friend. He lived for three hours, semi-conscious. He was a handsome youth with a long, narrow scar that started over one eye and ran down his cheek to his upper lip. It made his Arab face more handsome in a sinister way, but his eyes were warm and his smile was innocent and soft.

I used to borrow his brand new TR-4 during my last four weeks in Officer Candidate School. We had been buddies for a long time. We were young NCOs in the Tenth Special Forces Group and we believed intensely in what we stood for. I'll always remember him and still believe in what we believed in then. He would have felt the same way had I been the one to go first. The sacrifice was correct and acceptable.

Death Is...

Sounds and sights,
Strangers to my eyes and ears,
Rumble, come, stop briefly,
And then move on.

The graves of my companions are dug,
Embedded...filled,
Silently lamented over,
And soon forgot.

My mind is feverish and finds no rest;
Like tormented captives of a thousand hells,
It rages on and cries out in despair for reason
But finds at best—nothing!

I live although I'm dead;
No! not with fear,
nor with regret!
I saw him hit, and now he, too, is dead.

A paratrooper died this noon;
He was young; he did not fear.
His guts were spilled, and it made me sick.
His face grew pale, he screamed in pain but did not cry.

His eyes were dry; so were mine,
As he squeezed my hand in the agony of parting.
While the light bulbs flashed and there was cheer and clover,
Because at home, the football game was over.

South of Gian Than, January 1966

To the soldiers of the Fifth Special Forces Group the war consisted mostly of combat patrols. Normally, there were only two Americans on these patrols with a number of Vietnamese CIDG (Civil Indigenous Defense Group—irregulars—recruited from the local population) whose language few of us spoke, and many of whom were actually Viet Cong. The purpose of these patrols was ambush, and they sometimes went on for a week, far from base camp. The PRC-25 (our main radio) had a limited range, so we were soon out of communication with our camps. We were alone.

If a man got wounded, we stayed with him. This usually meant that the entire patrol went "missing in action." Sometimes the night sky would be so clear that you could almost touch the stars or read a map by moonlight. And a fresh breeze from the Gulf of Siam, ten miles to the west, would make the air cool, keep the mosquitoes down, and make the night pleasant for dying.

Ambush

Moonlight passing,
Encompassing
all the mute, sleepy scenes below,
Casting ghostly shadows in a silver, pale and bloodless glow,
Leaving me with empty feelings, loath to move or to stop,
Tired of staying, long past desire of another place to go.

Slowly in the pale light my hand moves over a metal disc,
it's the selector switch.
Back is safe, up is semi, forward is automatic.
A streak of infernal automatic tracer light will either miss
its mark
Heaven forbid! Or forgive me, Lord
and send my brother to hell or into your eternal bliss.

This lament of a ghostly ambush night,
Paling moon and mute starlight.
Witness the hunt.
Man seeks man, fear fights fear, savage, strange delight!
Stupefying fear of death or disfigurement
wishes death upon another just like me.
I ask God what my final punishment will be.

Then, Brother, you cross my sights.
You, who'll see your soul ascending or rejected to hell
downfalling
We are more alike than those who sent us to the rendezvous.
Lit by mute stars, speechless as by horror, witnessed by the
moon, so pale, so blue,
I kill you!

November 1966

My proudest day (next to the day I became an American citizen) was the day I put on the Green Beret—an unauthorized piece of headgear in the Army at the time. During my years of initiation and incessant training at Bad Toelz in Bavaria, Majors Bill Simpson III and Ralph Puckett, and Master Sergeants Barkhoff and Kaville taught me operational and technical skills and built my confidence. Through their matchless example they instilled in me the very special rules for ethical conduct expected of the best soldiers our country had. These rules were the rules that Colonel Aaron Bank had set down as the first colonel to command the Tenth Special Forces Group Airborne (Green Berets), a unit he organized, trained, and led. The unit crest was a large silver Trojan horse with a lightning bolt behind it. I have never wanted anything as much as I wanted to be a part of that group of men. Never before have I had to work as hard to prove my worth (it took two years of disapprovals and one Article 15—nonjudicial punishment). No promotion, commission, or award since then has even come close to the feeling I had when I put on my Green Beret—only a kid of twenty-three.

The friendships that were forged there remain forever tied in brotherhood. We were not paragons of virtue, although it must be said that we dug a lot of wells, built a lot of schools and hospitals, and cured a lot of sick people. We also went out in twos and threes and were never heard from again. We killed and were killed. We were bad and we were good. But just to have spent one tour in an A-Detachment (the basic Special Forces operational unit) made us heroes in our own eyes. What the rest of the world thought, thinks, or will think, really doesn't matter. This poem is for all my buddies—alive or dead—may they live forever.

To a Special Forces Soldier

Dive into the cold blue crystal,
and the sapphire of existence shall envelop
and soothe the heated soul.

Before the bell's last call,
in the greying early dawn,
before the birds awaken,
the columns of the guys and I
into the deep grass are taken
by feet aching and weary of the march.
The eastern sky yearns for the day
and reddens as if to say,
"Soon, young Special Forces Soldier,
Soon dead on the ground you'll lay.
Alone save for one more by your side
far, far away from friend and child and bride.
Distant from the happy crowds
the citizens at home, who dance, rejoice and chant
while the gong to early prayer sounds and echoes into the
distant misty swamp."

Is it a prayer or a warning for the Viet Cong in his camp?
a distant mound on which a sleepy sentry
his lonely vigil keeps.
Early, warns the prayer gong, before the daylight sweeps
aside the silky curtain of the night
an American patrol into tall grass vanishes from sight.

Oh how I wish that I could still…
that gong, that bell
that could sentence us to hell.
Oh how I want to run and hide
but there's another by my side
who'll never see me cringe with fear

but is as scared as I inside
so on we march with quickened stride
into the swamp where the Viet Cong preside.

The crystal blue of existence shall recall
that we were once here too.
The empty streets on Smoke Bomb Hill
The buildings gone, shall remember still
The toasts we drank when we were young
The tears uncried our laughs did hide.
We swore, we fought,
The furniture at the Annex we bought,
and those nasty souvenirs some of us caught.
And then...a jaunty farewell kiss
To woman and child, so many times!
The others stood in waiting groups
in tans and boots, bereted good looks
and gazed with glee at any sign of tears
Soldiers had no sentiments, no fears.
And then, that last long telephone call
from San Francisco or Travis Air Force Base
the line was long before the booth—"Hurry babe,
hurry, I gotta make one more call, just one more call."

Then we cried, two babies with no crib
And tore our hearts, for our love was strong and true.
And those minutes when the phone rang at Bragg
were like an ocean, deep and deep and blue.
Every silent pause when we didn't know what to say
meant our love was strong and true to the final dying day,
Why we wanted to fight so far away was hard to say
so we went our way,
and so we went and flew away
and blew away
and our brothers wore the Green Beret.

Those with whom we tore to shreds
the curtains on the Annex walls—
at Valinco's we would all sit, or
at the Sporting Bar someone would spit
into the beer of some Green Beret,
and steel our nerves for the days to come,
then head out to Plei Me or Tra Bong,
to dive into the blue sapphire
the blue crystal of existence.

February, 1968

What can I say about malaria, except that whenever the fever gets up to 105 degrees, Dengue (or Black Water Fever as it is called in some parts) cuts in. In the delirium of a sustained high fever, everything turns and twists in the mind and is amplified: past experiences, hurts given and received, no letters from the loved one. The contemplation of war and its sounds are vivid and confusing. The faces of war are scary, particularly the faces of the callous and the cruel, be they our own or theirs, and the faces of the fearful and apprehensive prisoners. Then there are the faces of the compassionate and kind. The chivalrous manly face of the First Sergeant who, miraculously, in the middle of nowhere, in the dead of night, produces a bottle of Old Grand Dad just for you. That, and a bottle of aspirins, gets you through the night and the fever.

Malaria Attack

Within the pit of darkness and despair,
The bottomless depth of tearing fantasy that is my gut,
I sleep,
Let it rain; let the lightning flash,
And let the thunder roll.
Wake my tortured brain and stormy soul;
Let passion pour and fire sweep;
Look at myself.
I am now and was asleep.
Large drops of rain I thought were tears
Blind my waking eyes; they're hot
Could rain be hot?
No; it's only the rain of some tropic night.
Wake, wake; there are no dreams; stir to life.
Awake like lava, hot with spitting rocks,
Passion of flaming orange red, white with heat—
Now divorced from all illusion.
My feverish brain is racked…
Near diffusion, self-destructing—
No longer able to hold all the pain and sorrow.
Who knows how much more fear and pain will hold tomorrow?

Good Morning World (Vietnam)

This morning I feel like a worm on the manure pile
of a German farm yard

Sticking my head out of a pile of shit
to give this world a "once over."

The weather isn't all that good;
I see a bunch of green flies having breakfast.

Spring 1968

Trying to remember what Michael's full name was, I took out the old company roster and also looked at my diary. I had written in Michael's (leader of the third platoon) name by hand, so he couldn't have been with the company more than a couple of days before he died. I will never forget him, and every evening I say a prayer for him. He was a good shepherd and a good leader.

After we were ambushed, the company point (three man forward patrol) was wiped out except for Penson. He had lost his weapon and was hiding, bleeding to death, a hundred yards away in a bamboo thicket on the opposite shore of the Bo river. A North Vietnamese Battalion was also dug-in there, well camouflaged in four-meter-thick bunkers that had been built by the Viet Minh in the early fifties. A palm forest had grown over the bunkers, so they were barely visible and virtually untouchable. In the withering fire to our front, the water of the river churned like there was a tropical storm. I was pinned down myself beside a young, dead machine gunner at the river's edge, and saw Michael swimming across the river in plain view of the enemy. We gave all the fire support we could muster with three rifle squads, but other platoons were fighting around us and were in trouble too, drawing off support.

I saw Michael reach Penson, grab him, and start back. Penson was bleeding, but he was hanging on. Meanwhile, our company was being hit hard to the rear. Michael and Penson almost made it back; they were cut down ten yards from our sand bar. I put Michael in for the Medal of Honor, but it was downgraded to a Silver Star. Still, it doesn't matter much. In my heart he lives with Penson and the company point, and I remember them every night when I say the kaddish.

14

The First Psalm

(Dedicated to Michael, a Platoon Leader)

Oh Lord, the fighting rages all around me and
I am lying prostrate before my enemies.
The bullets of their guns seek my heart
And their mortars hunger for my flesh.
Oh Lord, my master, I am alone
My Shepherd sits at Thy side
but I am in fear and He hears not my voice.
My companions are dying and laid low,
hear my prayer in this hour of fear.
You, whose magnificence and power
Cannot be challenged in the Existence.
Save me and mine, from the wrath and hatred of our enemies.
they are like packs of ravenous wolves,
And seek the destruction of my body and soul.
Do not let their bullets find me,
Nor their malicious tongues hurt my name and spirit.
Have mercy on my companions and me
And give us victory, because it pleases Thee to do it.
That I may ever know Thy will and might
And that, I may ever praise Thy name before the heathen.
Let them know Thy power and be bewildered by it.
Do not let them harm me Lord
I am naked and cannot help myself.
All mercy and forgiveness comes from You.
Give my Shepherd leave to rescue me and my companions.
Don't leave us at their mercy when I call to Thee.

March 1968

From Camp Evans and Quang Tri City we started south along Highway 555, the "Street Without Joy" of the French Union Forces of fifteen years before. We fought for every acre of land towards Hue City. It rained and was terribly cold. I kept having attacks of malaria and Dengue, but did not go on sick call. We were the 501st Parachute Infantry; the North Vietnamese called us "soldiers of the terrible little bird" because of our screaming eagle shoulder patches, which were the insignia of our parent unit, the 101st Airborne Division. The North Vietnamese and the Viet Cong were also hard, tough, and devoted to their cause. We were the best our country had. We were not fanatics, nor particularly hard and callous, but were brave and healthy, and truly believed in stopping communism.

"T-Bone" was a mountaintop where we placed one of our many artillery bases to support the infantry while clearing the area of the enemy. It was a wonderful feeling to be under the umbrella of such a fire base because when we got into trouble all we needed to do was call and help was on the way (in Special Forces such a luxury was rare), and we were always in trouble. The rifle companies fought alone rather than as battalions, so we were always outnumbered.

We discovered that the North Vietnamese soldier was as much a stranger here as we were. He was very young, could and did get lost, was not good at reading maps, and did not always hit what he shot at. Moreover, he was scared as hell of us because of the propaganda he received in his indoctrination. One miserable rainy day we took a break for a smoke and a cup of coffee. Where I sat, the rain began to uncover a mass grave of North Vietnamese soldiers. In the tropics, decay comes quick. I wondered who they were, and if their families would ever know what became of them.

T-Bone

His large, black eyes looked expressionless at me,
As though my friends and I were nothing much to see.
Their grinning faces expressed the same old view
That in this "New World," there is nothing really new.

Both they and we had made an arduous journey,
They on foot, we on plane and ship.
We all hunt fate, or is fate the actual hunter?
Did we decide, or were we the ones he'd whip?

I pause with wonder; no one said a word.
His helmet was of some cheap stuff of which we never heard.
But it bothered me that it should be on crooked;
So I bent down, and with one hand I took it.

I'm somewhat shaken looking at his clothing.
It's dirty, muddy, all covered up with clay.
Thank God his friends at home don't see it;
A soldier in such a state would surely cause dismay!

I suppose you sang some songs when you left home.
Your uniform was freshly washed and pressed.
Your dear Mother's hand did tremble just a little
As she with silent tears a blessing o'er you said.

Your wife you watched with aching heart as she, the anxious
minutes with small talk tried to fill.
"Ngoc, take some more rice; we have enough to last;
Here, take this shawl. Do you need some more cigarettes?
The journey's long. Be sure to get your rest."

Yes, I think you sang a song; so did all of you.
Did you really think all you were told was true?
Did you believe all the things they said?
That you'd march South and by cheering crowds be met.

17

Your kind down here all, want you to come down
To free the farmers and the merchants, too.
The fisherman will welcome your arrival.
And share with joy his daily catch with you.

But when you came, no cheering crowds you greeted.
The folks you met feared you much more than us,
For although they had but little love for us,
All things must pass—as our short stay, too, must!

Oh, yes; they know that all things one day end,
And we who came, will someday go away.
But you came to preach some brand new type of glory,
The kind which turns all bright things into gray.

Sometimes we do seem odd to them down here;
But, hell…at least we laugh and joke when we have time.
They laugh at us, but also laugh with us.
Sorrow and grief are not a constant stay.

"Why do you bring with you this sorrow, to a land where happy
people dwell?"
I know it's no use asking questions; even if you knew, you'd
never tell.
There is a stench of death…disintegration.
Wherever you march explodes the cannon's shell.

Yet, I see your grinning faces and know you're saying,
"We'll soon be with you, too."
When you departed this great path of sorrow
I guess you never knew what hit you.
Like a serpent in the grass, death jumped up and bit you.
Was your grave the heaped mound of a stray One-Seven-Five?
Or did the guys left alive bury you beneath this paddy dike?
Which now the monsoon rain did wash—
Revealing your skeletons; your flesh had turned to dust.

Tell me; I think we're much alike.
"Did you die quickly or in searing agony?
Have you been dead for long as you are waiting here for me?
Or did the worms clean your bones so splendidly?"

Well, rest your bones old friend, while I will smoke a
cigarette and talk awhile.
This killing is such tiring business; at home they're not even
interested.
Sometimes they even watch us die, after a day's work, on
television…
Drinking beer or eating apple pie!

I, too, have a child I love beyond compare and had a wife I
love more than myself.
But she took another; the waiting for a soldier is too much
bother.
And love I found is just a word that's said
For getting someone quicker into bed…no more!

I really wish your grinning skull could talk;
I know you'd have a handsome tale or two.
My guys and I are just like the five of you.
Hate? Hell, us? Given a chance we'd have been friends—
pretty good ones, too!

It's a strange world, you know. If it's not this, then it's
another.
There are many who did not come, you know; some had too
much money or possessions; the athletes and politicians, to
name a few.
Some even fled with the stench of fear behind them—claiming
their beliefs the cause.
Ah, yes; there are the excuses. Duty rests but with a chosen
few.

And, so, the flower of the finest youth goes off to serve
as men are wont to do; and die, or lose an arm and leg or eyes
While the ones who stay behind breed more of their kind—
not like you.
For your bones are cold,
And your seed was like the dew.

Which at the warming of the rising sun,
Hangs but awhile on some green blades of grass—
Then, like the sparkling of a distant star,
Evaporates…in the early morning mist to join the ether.

Spring, 1968

When we were hit, I had gone to the head of the column and was chewing out a machine gunner for not carrying his weapon at the ready. The fire was so intense that my web gear got singed. The machine gunner and the recon sergeant got it at the same time. Stupefied by the fire's intensity, I continued to key down on my hand set. I had been talking to the Battalion Command Post. I babbled for what seemed an eternity, and I'm embarrassed to think about it now. The first sergeant tackled me and I went down hard. A lifetime later I found myself out of machine-gun ammo, and some guy was trying to hit me with an RPG (Soviet made rocket propelled grenade). Luckily, he had only armor piercing rounds, so only the soles of my jungle boots got burned.

As I rolled onto my back, I saw a chopper shove ammo boxes out in the center of our perimeter about one hundred yards away. Everybody was running low on ammo. Everett Doolittle dashed for the chopper under incredibly dense automatic fire, grabbed four cans of M-60 machine-gun ammo, and ran towards me. He almost got to me before he received a machine-gun burst into his stomach and kidneys. With his last strength, as he fell towards me, he hurled the ammo boxes at me. I crawled up to him, cried for the medic, and started to drag him to cover. He was very young, about eighteen or so, with clear blue eyes. As I grabbed his arm to pull him, he looked me in the eyes and, gritting his teeth, said, "That's okay, Sir. I'll make it. I'm Airborne." He started to crawl, but couldn't. The medic and first sergeant took him away and I returned my attention to the urgent business at hand. I pray for him and all the rest who fell that day. And if by chance Doolittle lived, then may this little psalm give him grace and Godspeed on his journey through life.

The Second Psalm

Time has come to praise thee Lord,
Enough of my frightened cries for Thy help this afternoon.
Enough of my cries for assistance and grace.
Time for the kaddish and songs of praise to Thee Lord most high.
My companions, brave and beautiful youth
Have kept faith true to their belief in Thee and our country.
They stood their ground and fought like men.
Either to live or die as You decreed this day.
I hear the sound of the Choppers coming
To carry them away, and to bring things we need,
Perhaps a letter from home to me.
Those of us alive, are silent in our thoughts.
Who knows what we think except You.
You read our thoughts and You read our hearts.
You know the vibrations of our very souls.
Our uniforms are dirty, torn, shredded,
We are covered with the blood of our enemies
As we are with the blood of our companions and brothers
But we are all companions and warriors of the sacrifice
Of those who sent us here to test our hearts and our faith.
Praise be Thine therefore Our Father, Lord of Hosts.
God of Abraham, Isaac and Jacob, and glory to be Yours even as
Our Lord Jesus Thy Only Son taught us to glorify Thee.
Let me sing in my heart, Gaudens, Gaudens to Thee
As we sang them in the arenas of Rome.
There too Thy will stood supreme,
Fulfilled in the New and Everlasting Covenant You promised us
Thru Your servants Jeremiah, Isaiah and Elijah and all of
Your messengers, and gavest us through our Lord Jesus.
Our enemies are now no longer cruel, they rest now
They too are handsome youth, brave to the end.
They too are like the spotless lambs brought to Thy altar.
Lord God, do not forget the promise of Jesus Thy Son
Give a few chambers to them, in the many mansions of Thy kingdom.

After all they were true to the end, when so very few played the man.
Let all of our voices sing praises to Thee
And let me give Thee praise and thanksgiving
For giving me courage to stay and fight and not to run away.
And for letting me live this afternoon to praise Thee
And letting me write one more letter home.

Nui Tha Nhan, August 1968

It was hot and humid. The rains of the monsoon had drifted and Hue was free again—of the Viet Cong and NVA that is. Hue was a beautiful and noble city with cultured, reserved, and dignified people. It had a beautiful cathedral, and Father Pelsemaker, S.J.(Society of Jesus), was trying, along with the surviving priests and nuns, to gather the orphans in order to clothe and feed them. We found the rest of the priests and nuns buried in mass graves around the city. Infantrymen don't do that sort of thing—mass killings I mean—so I could never believe that North Vietnamese Infantrymen would have done it. It was the work of the local party committee and the Viet Cong execution squads.

With several detached teams from the 501st Parachute Infantry we reorganized, retrained, and re-equipped the local Regional and Popular Force companies (RF/PF)—something like our National Guard—because in most places they had been destroyed. I had been assigned to the Thua Thien district, and it was the only district that had not collapsed. Because they had a good leader, the RF/PF troops, as ill-equipped as they were, hung in there and fought off the finest North Vietnamese infantry. The troop's leader was an ex-Viet Minh infantry officer, who after the defeat of the French, decided that there was no room for the non-communist in the Viet Minh, and had gone south. Although he was neither Buddhist nor Christian, he cared for his people, and labored for them tirelessly. He was a district chief, but far too unselfish and chivalrous to become a general of the Republic of South Vietnam. He remains a hero forever to me, and to his people.

I had participated in the fighting for the citadel of Imperial Hue. I watched the cameras of UPI, AP, Agence France Presse, and others on

25

top of the MACV (Military Advisory Command Vietnam) compound, taking pictures for the evening news. They took close-ups of a dying young marine as though interviewing some kid leaving Wrigley Field after a game. I asked myself why, but didn't dare to ask the others. Somehow I always felt that not enough newsmen died in combat, the way our guys had to. But they made more money than we did, so maybe they had more to live for.

So, one day, in the heat of noon, sitting on the sandbagged roof of my bunker on top of the hill "Nui Tha Nhan," I wrote "Ur." This was only the midpoint of my Indochina sojourn, and I intended to complete the pilgrimage or die trying. The imperial citadel, the city and its people, moved me to write "Ur" with a clear mind and heart. It reflects deeply my roots, my culture, and my beliefs.

Ur

Gently swaying shadows moved once
Upon a golden sea of grain.
Endlessly the gilded ocean,
Stretched across the ancient plain.
Now the desert sand does shift
With the changing of the wind,
twenty of one hundred score...
that's how long the grain has gone,
This is the time as I recall
Looking on this ancient wall.
Which too, was built long after.

The forger's bench, the heat of noon,
The anvil of the golden orb.
Ceaselessly my spirit molds
With vicious heat my mind unfolds.
The heat does etch, the cleaver splits
No sound this mighty roar emits.
But in the mute noise of the fire
Sears and tears my soul entire,
As if a meal upon it planned
My soul has backed upon the sand
Before the bells to vespers.

From the misty, distant line
Crags lift up, that once bore wine.
The hot wind on its silent feet
Brings me the tone of soundless bells
As the foes of bygone days
Announced their threats with silver chimes
That decorated mail and steed
Dancing, prancing on the grain.

The bells resound without a tone
And echo through deserted halls
Over dusty altars.
Where no Mass has long been said,
Where the spider weaves his web,
Where no candles ever burn.
There the bones in dusty urns
Await the Judgement Hour—

Time flew once as water ran,
Now it sleeps upon the sand.
Upon the Earth Him they denied
As before, Him they abused.
Too great in glory did they feel
The Masters of the Evening Sky,
Life and Death, Call and Send
Upon the bleached sand they fell.
Their tears dried quick upon their cheeks
In empty desolation.

Now only the fly and such as he
Lend their unwelcome company
to me.
On my journey through this Land.
From Uruk to Samarkand.
Time, Where are you?
Sweet dawns of the dew-kissed grain
Palmy scented sunsets, fled
have buried yourselves within these blocks
Behind the moat of comprehension.

Throughout empty hours, pregnant with dreams
Now racing along swiftly…then still, unmoving.
At times the Ghibili, then
Silent, bleak, empty.
Like a glass house without windows
A theater without a stage or door

This anthill without ants
Is like this highway without a traveler
Leading from nowhere to unknown destinations.

Is this the pier on polluted waters,
From where there is no place to flee?

"Ecce Homo!"
Have you no wisdom or compassion?
A will for understanding?
Where that should have been…
The heart for it was lacking.

"Ubinam gentium sumus." And the sound
of water still trickles from the hands,
then, The Testament was changed within all Lands.
That He would not, thought they
His vengeance take
And wreak destruction in His judgement's wake.
So did they change…though He unchanging is.

The journey's long, the pause like decades spent,
Dust devils rise from the sand, to witness my torment.
But I burned my incense early, ere the night
From the scorching countenance of the sun took flight.
And sped on upon my shiny midnight steed
From the twin water course I lead.
Towards Antioch, where I once bled.

I stop just briefly in this fiery glow
to look upon these walls and battlements.
The moat echoes silent, bygone screams
As the drawbridge fell and with it these
Who now awake in my reflection.
Though they thought, He did not need to think
Ever true to His promise, He gave them wine to drink.
He did not leave, though all did turn away

Ignoring their faith on that fateful day.
So I pause now, to see this place of old.

Upon the river's bank now flows the mud
North from Cyrus' tomb into the crags I must
To seek a people strong of heart and bold.
For there oh Ur your ancient children dwell
who did not change and accept as dictates fell.
But chancing fiery Hell, they kept their noble ways
The horsemen return to Ur from whence they came.

Lord, your servant goes alone.
Fall he does many times,
But You lift him up again and again.
You never tire in Your forgiveness
Never tire of listening to his excuses
Why he falls short of the promises he makes;
Nay, the promises he breaks before You.
Unworthy and undeserving of Your grace
Of the rewards and gifts You bestow on him. He is made of the
mud under Your sandals.
Yet Love You he does, Lord, beyond the reach of words.

No treasures known, would he exchange
For the place of a grain of sand under Your footstool.
How could he?
For Lord of Heaven and Host Thou art
But to Thy servant a Father.
Feared and worshiped Thou art,
But Thy servant Loves Thee.
He eats not alone, but banquets in Thy presence.
The piece of rock-hard bread in his hands,
Is sweet loaf with poppy seeds
Fresh from the baker's oven,
Because he eats it in Thy company.

This glass of water is a cup of the finest wine,
He offers it to Thee, and his heart overflows with joy.
He sings Thy praises among the silent hills,
Along empty river beds and mute forests.
Sing and dance he does to Thy glory.

No farmer or merchant this, Thy servant.
A warrior he, whom Thou hast blessed.
An unworthy son who loves his Father,
Surrendered, without reservations to Thee.
Guard him, dost Thou, in the valley of the A Shau
Thy shield keeps him from harm.
Thy sword silently and swiftly falls,
Like a swarm of bees protecting their hive.
Glorious the heavens
where Thy palace and Thy throne do stand,
Amid the splendor of Thy stars.
The desert blooms, and ice fields yield their grip to Thy flowers
And Thou layest the velvet grass under Thy servant's naked feet
Like a carpeted stairway to Thy altar.

Mountains curtained in blue silk
These the walls of Thy temple.
How could not everything pale before Thy glory
All of this is the work of Thy hands.
Let the blood of His servant be worthy,
And pure in the eyes of the Lord.
May it be acceptable as the sacrifice
He brings to his Father through his existence.
The Lord grant him grace and speed him on his quest,
His Father guide him on this journey for His own sake.
Let the tree that the servant planted for the glory
Of the Lord, fulfill its purposes.

1968

There were too many times that those of us who made it thought we never would. After surviving many times, I felt like saying prayers in public, but didn't for fear of offending others. Whenever I had the time, I'd say my act of contrition. I would say it out of fear at times, but mostly out of love. If there was occasion, I'd wash myself so that if I died, I would die clean. I got used to this ritual in the Special Forces A-Camp because I had time for reflection before a patrol. All in all, it's difficult to imagine what a soldier thinks, or if he prays, but there were many among the ones I met who did pray then, and still do.

Thank You

In the silence of my world,
I light my candles
Before Your Throne oh Lord.
I burn my incense
Before Your stars at night
And in the pink reflection
Of Your wakening sun.
And when it rains, oh Lord,
I sing my praises
For every drop of rain that falls,
For they bless the earth
Where now I roam,
And where once You walked.
My heart rejoices with happiness
When I behold Your glory,
In all that You have fashioned
And for letting me walk among them.

Zaragoza, Spain, Fall 1967

All the members of the A and B Detachments had known each other for many years. We thought ourselves lucky to be posted back to the Tenth Special Forces Group in Bad Toelz, Germany. It was, to be sure, better than Fort Bragg or Fort Benning, but it was not as we had remembered it. Gone were the super Special Forces officers we had grown to admire, love, and respect, like Ben Ivey and Bill Simpson. The few serious men remaining like Don Campbell, couldn't find their bearings easily, because although we were good fighters fresh from the A-Camps of Vietnam, we had not yet learned the finer things, such as the politics of being a successful officer. The NCOs (in Special Forces every enlisted detachment member was an NCO) were of course, still around, and all of us, commissioned or non-commissioned, were happy to be alive and seeing each other again.

In the summer of 1967, we deployed to Spain for a big exercise. The drop zone was changed on us several times in flight so that we'd really have to earn our pay. While en route (it was a long flight in C-130s), we reminisced and told war stories as soldiers always do. I began to write a poem called "Hello Charley," which I finished on the ground.

The "Charley the Tuna" advertisement of the time was very popular with the guys in my team, who referred to the Viet Cong as "Charley." The Viet Cong, like "Charley the Tuna," were in many ways the true tragicomic figures of the war. Their finest units were sacrificed ruthlessly by General Giap who took advantage of their incredible bravery, commitment, and loyalty. So when the war finally ended, the Viet Cong could not defend their country from the foreign occupiers from the North. I also knew a few good Viet Cong. I suppose there should have been hate in me for them, but I just couldn't come up with it.

We did not have many airborne operations in Vietnam, except for the 503rd Parachute Infantry (a unit of the 173rd Airborne Brigade), which jumped against the Viet Cong in a combat operation called "Junction City." But we did have some Mike Force (special reaction force) parachute drops and special jumps that were not recognized as combat jumps by the Army nor will ever compare to the likes of Corregidor, Sicily, Normandy, or the Rhine. Being a paratrooper on my way to Spain, and at least for a while not having to worry about being shot at, I was moved to write this poem. It does have a certain sense of comic irony and that really is what the life of a fighter is all about.

Hello Charley

(Dedicated to the 173rd Airborne Brigade)

Ghostly hostile shadows dwell
before the inky night without—
the gaping door a way to Hell
just one more route
just one more well.

On the elevator down to hell
lit by some infernal glow—
a final tale I long to tell
before I go, before we fell.

I took some boys out for a blast
to pound upon the Devil's door—
kick Cerberus' doggie ass
break the Boatman's steady oar
and win ourselves a ten day pass.

We'd all come back after the fight
across the River Styx we'd swim—
a grin or two on faces tight
"Are you afraid inside like him?"
"Not me," "No way," "Hey I'm all right!"

In the red glow of the troop door light
I can see the form of the static lines—
wildly twisting in the night
while on the ground by jungle vines
squats Tuna Charley out of sight.

A pure delight his ass to kick
a damned fine fighter, the Tuna, he—
if he spots this drop I'm dead meat quick
Still I must jump, I do and see
his weapon flash as moments tick.

A buddy takes a hit below
his parachute is now his shroud—
lifeless head bobs to and fro
in a furrow newly plowed
he comes to rest where food will grow.

Charley Tuna, jungle kills
leaves you with no time to mourn—
speech like wind, movements still
we meet like ghosts before the dawn
and test the Lord's unchanging will.

December 1968

While driving across the country, I visited a friend in Abbeville, Louisiana. We had become friends in 1958 at basic training. During basic, he'd let me use his '57 Crown Victoria coupe whenever my '53 Packard convertible broke down. At that time, he was far from home, and whenever we got a long weekend, he'd come home with me and spend it with my family. When I next saw him, in 1968, he had settled down to civilian life with a nice family of his own.

He complained how dull life had become for him. Things at home were either too boring or too stressful. "You don't understand what it's like. You can go to war, you have adventure. Life for us is nothing but a daily routine." He was surprised that I could not relate to his life.

But things had also changed for me. My parents were divorced, so I had no "hometown" left. Like so many other countless guys who had gone to Vietnam, my marriage was barely hanging in there, and I was going back to Nam after a thirty day furlough. I had barely seen my family, and when we were together we quarreled. I could not express to my friend or family the things I felt inside about the war and my alienation from Americans, who didn't understand the very ideals we fought for. For many of us, that alienation never ceased.

The Wanderer

Oh, Wanderer; for I see you are a stranger here;
Your worn out garments and your dusty shoes
Speak of a lengthy journey.
Tell me of the distant lands, of their peoples,
And their customs, the sparkling seas,
Of golden sands and desert storms,
Of jungles green, of lands with snowcapped mountains
Tell of the sights you've seen.
Just tell me all at random.
I, too, long to take to wings
And also see the places far,
The roads on which you travelled there.
Just travel on without a care;
Just travel on at random.
My heart is strong; it beats with ease.
My eyes are clear and longing
To behold all you have seen,
And laugh and live as you have done,
Just living life and seeing things,
Like a blue bird on his wings,
Like a clock on pendulum swings,
And watch time on its glorious course, just living life at random.
Oh, Traveler; come in and stay awhile,
And tell me of your wondrous life,
Your freedom and good fortune.
Relax and take your burden off,
And sit down by my fire.
If you're too tired to tell your tales,
Rest now; you can tell them later.
I wish that I could have lived life,
and felt all things that you have felt—
Leaving my footprints on the road.
I would be so much wiser.
But wisdom comes with many miles,

And truth is learned with tear-filled tries.
No laughter ever stays unchanged.
The searing sun and desert wind,
Will carve deep furrows in your skin,
Your hair is bleached at first to gold,
But hot winds and the northern cold
will turn the gold to silver.

I thank you, Friend, for food and rest.
For the warmth of your bright fire,
And I shall rest.

Then I'll tell my tale of distant lands.
Of sparkling seas,
Of the glorious life,
of freedom's ease.
but pardon me, dear Friend, oh please,
Don't be led abroad from these;
This house, this hearth,
Your neighbors close,
Don't choose to live a life like mine;
Unless you drink my bitter wine,
Don't live a life at random.

Summer 1969

At dusk, as the last rays of light began to fade, the company made ready for the night: Blacken the face and hands, check magazines, zero-fire machine guns, rifles, and grenade launchers, and issue the last patrol orders. We knew that the North Vietnamese were watching us as we made our nightly preparations, and that could not be helped. There were twenty meters between each soldier while they got ready for the night patrols, and that made the 110 guys in the valley look like a whole battalion. When the sun set and it was almost dark, a cheer went up from every throat, "Airborne! Airborne! All the way!" I was amazed at this display of enthusiasm. We had the North Vietnamese on the run, but they weren't beaten, so we continued to take casualties. One night, out of so many countless nights, Yamashita fell while on patrol. With him went Reyes and Santos. Their memories are always with me as I say the kaddish.

We used to hold "rap sessions" at the squad level to ease the tension. At first it was tough. The guys balked, but then it became easier. During one of these, one of the riflemen threw a copy of the "Stars and Stripes" down at my feet and screamed, "Why in the hell should we die? Why me? I don't give a damn...nobody here does!" I picked up the paper, which had Jane Fonda's picture on it. I wish I still had it, that paper. The guys had a way of backing me into a corner during these "rap sessions." I blurted out, "This is the 503rd Parachute Infantry! We're the last paratroopers our country has in this fight! If we don't keep the faith, who will?" I really will never know what made me say those words, but the answer was, "Wow, Man! Right on! All the way, Sir!" It changed things, And if these words last for a while, and if some of the guys who made the parachute assault on the island of Corregidor during World War II read these words, think! Maybe the guys at Dak To and in the Anh Loa were not the heroes in the eyes of the country that you were, but they lived and died like heroes, and they brought honor to our regiment.

Honor

I stood in awe to see them go;
So I too, did walk along.
In prime of youth, we chosen few
Upon the holy Altar given.
So many hearts for freedom's sake!
Our blood our precious essence make
The red stripes sparkle on your field.
Our love for you, those pure, white ribbons be,
to grace your masts, to grace all staffs eternally.
When evening blue awakes the stars,
Look up; you'll see us standing there.
When others condemned our beloved land,
Disdained the letters which mean MEN,
We were true to you, beloved flag.
You just look into the heavens.

August 1969

This was a terribly hard and hot patrol. We had run out of water, although everybody carried four canteens. The mountains were steep and high and the weight of our equipment was incredible. I called the battalion CP (command post) and asked what the temperature was. The reply was, "one-two-zero degrees." Our German Shepherd scout dog was useless and going crazy from the heat, even though everybody except the machine gunners carried extra water for him. His name was "King" and his handler loved him. The choppers tried to drop water cans, but the foliage was too thick, and the crevasses so steep that we could not find them.

Finally, after ten hours or so, we reached a clearing on top and the chopper came with water and food, and mail. As usual, there was no letter for me. As I stood, looking over the valleys below, I kept thinking about grape soda and how wonderful it would be to drink a bottle of it, ice cold. That was my favorite pop when I used to caddy at the Worthington Golf Club in Parkersburg as a kid. Thinking about grape soda and summer in West Virginia and my very innocent youth, for a moment my soul, in sadness, took me on a little pilgrimage across the Ohio river to Marrieta, Ohio. Luckily, "Charley" (the VC) was just as hot as we were and we made no contact.

Elizabeth Anne

Balmy summer afternoons when dreams were three, four dozen
golf balls found in the creek by the 18th hole green.

Hot summer afternoons of idle hours in the shade of the caddy
Shack when a dream was a double caddy for 18 holes with a
fifty-cent tip from each golfer.

Then after the ninth hole my tongue drug on the parched grass
and my fifteen year old back was killing me.
It was then that I dreamed.
I dreamed I was kissing you.
Your lips were like cold grape soda and I loved you so much.

That night I shared with you my love
popcorn, a coke and a quart of strawberries,
and a movie with Esther Williams.
You ran your beautiful hands over my crew cut head.
I loved you.
Your eyes reflected in the floodlights
at halftime on Friday night.
I met you on the turf with a bouquet of roses,
and the band played "Varsity Drag."
You laughed.

Just wait…after the game!
I'll never forget your smile
how your red lips sparkled in the floodlights,
how the band played,
how you'd give me one flower at your father's house
after the game.

Balmy afternoons are now full of tropic jungle heat.
My back kills me still under the weight of a 65 pound pack
my rifle, my ammunition, my hand grenades.

My feet hurt, too. I think I'll die of thirst.
Thirst stirs memories of cold, grape soda,
of strawberries, and you,

Your lips were as red as the megaphone in your hands.
All glistened in the floodlights.
The sun reflects the dull, black glare of my weapon's muzzle.
Below, far below stretch the endless rice paddies.
Villages seen through heat waves.
Causing images of trees to bend
as I am bent before the weight of life.
I am thirsty, and now your memory comes back
and finds a way to reach me.
So far away. Strange after all this time
I might die thinking about you and cold, grape soda.

June 1969

It had been an average morning after an average night in the foothills of the Tiger Mountains. There had been the usual combat patrols. Each rifle squad was out, with one rifle squad close in for the security of the CP (command post). In the early dawn, the squads returned to the CP for breakfast and rest. As usual, there had been contact. In fact, Leon Strigotte's patrol had been ambushed just after sunset about a half mile from the CP. During this action, a very young kid, a grenadier who liked to be called "Alabama," (which I thought at first a little presumptuous and very funny) performed an incredible feat. Shooting with his M-79 grenade launcher in the darkness of the sparse forest at the muzzle flashes of the enemy machine guns and automatic rifles (AK-47s), at a distance of some fifty to sixty yards, he hit one enemy machine gunner in the chest, and another in the stomach, killing both. In the morning when they brought in the bodies of the young North Vietnamese infantrymen, I was taken by their youth. They were handsome and innocent looking in death.

That night, I put the company CP into the ruins of a burnt-out Catholic chapel and wrote this psalm. I suppose it sounds odd, but I will always believe in the continuity of being. One cannot cease to be a Christian when one becomes a soldier, and one cannot be a Christian without being an Old Testament Jew. There is to me something very fundamental in the love of God, in the love of the prophets, and in the fulfillment of the Redeemer, our Lord Jesus. So especially in war, the Christian must never forget what he is obliged to do: To fight like the lion, but in victory, to be compassionate and kind as the Lord taught us we must be, for it is in mercy that we are to "love our enemies."

The Third Psalm

In the silent darkness of Thy Temple, Oh Lord
I hear the chants of thanksgiving and praise.
Glorifying Thee for Thy works, for Thy magnificence and Mercy.
I smell the incense of purification
And the chains of the incense burner brushing gently against each
other,
Comes to the ears of my spirit, unheard by others.
My heart is enveloped by the warmth of Thy presence.
Bless those who long ago sang their praises to Thee in this place.
Bless those too who now sing their prayers to Thee in the mute hours
We are helpless and eternal children,
We never tire singing the Sanctus, and the Kyrie
For we were the children of many nations and could pray together
Only in the language of those who hated us as we bore witness to Thee
Loud hosannas resound in Thy Church
Whose roof is now the tropical sky.
Spilled over by the planets and stars
Which You placed there to please Thine eyes.
Look favorable on us, my companions and I
We claim not the knowledge of the World and its infinite mysteries.
But we put our trust in Thee, Lord, God Magnificent Creator.
Forget us not in the hour of our need when we call to Thee
As You did not withhold Your protection from our beloved David
When he appealed to You for help.
Accept this prayer to Thee as You accepted his.
Outside the heathen is about us, and we are alone and lonely.
Purify us for the coming fight this night Lord of Hosts.
Might is Thine, and we warriors are but babes on Our Father's Knee.
Keep us safe this night, and worthy of being called
Children of the Most High.
All honor and glory be Thine Forever. Amen.

January 1969

We'd only been married a short time, and it was wonderful. Then came the time of trials, brought on by my involvement in an unpopular war and the long combat tours it required. Our personal values were worlds apart and this became more apparent as the war dragged on. We knew we had the freedom to stay or leave and we tried with all our hearts to make it work. We tried to do that which was noble, honorable, just, and good, but our personal, physical, and material needs outweighed our ideals. "The Parting" was written sadly at the crossroads of two lives— when I was on the plane from Germany to Vietnam and ultimate stress was being placed on the marriage.

The Parting

Go, silently let your feet carry you away
And the sounds that were a part of mine
My world will fade like the clatter of the storks
Long before the snows of winter came.

Silence now covers my world like freshly fallen snow
Which long awaited, unexpectedly lies white upon the ground.
It is silent, as at all the graves and crosses,
Silence so far away, of a bygone day—still…

Go silently, it was no use.
Whatever you seek, I hope will come your way.
A warmth with wildflower fragrance
Will make your summer's day.

From whence you came, I did not know
Though somewhere we touched very long ago.
The chill that now with crystals sparkling sweeps
Enfolds like snow my gentle sorrow.

It grasps my heart…I'm sorry,
Although I should not be.
When I arrived, it was past your mid of night
I, in my early morning, passed in the greying light.

June 1969

I suppose that there really are no innocents. At least not in the sense that our media and press like to define the term "innocent civilian," because "civilians" are not innocent of anything. They, like the military, are people. But little children, children under the age of seven, are innocent, and in war are especially afraid and helpless. They love their parents without question and without reservation. The loss or abuse of their parents cuts into their little hearts. I always thought that the protection of these little frightened souls was the moral obligation of a soldier, especially an American soldier. On the ground, an infantryman sees much suffering close up. This is something an aviator or an artilleryman seldom sees.

Once, after we had driven a North Vietnamese element out of a hamlet, with burning huts everywhere and bodies lying in the streets, with women and kids screaming and crying in grief, a little five-year-old girl, with big, beautiful eyes came up to me. She asked if she could go and fill my canteen with water. So I gave her my canteen and she ran off. When she came back, I was sitting on the ground smoking a cigarette. I took a couple of Hershey's Tropical Chocolate bars from my rucksack, opened a can of C-rations, and gave them to her. She took the things, and sat quietly among all the din and chaos and ate the food, occasionally looking at me thoughtfully with those big brown eyes. Her face was beautiful. She was dirty and dusty and smoky and there were furrows in the dirt on her face that her tears had made.

After she finished eating her chocolate, she came a little closer, looking at me very intently. I was puzzled by this, but she kept looking into my eyes and inched closer and closer. Suddenly, she lunged at me, threw

51

her little arms around my neck, and kissed me. Just as suddenly, she jumped back, turned around, and ran away into the smoldering streets. If thirty months of combat left their mark on me, that little kiss made the pain and sacrifice worth it all.

To a Little Vietnamese Girl

I look at you and touch your eyes.
My fingers trace your cheeks
The path of your tears.
You have cried.
You have cried too often for just a child.
What can I do?
Wish I could have cried every tear for you.
Do you think I am strong and tall?
I carry fear with me.
Are you afraid, my child?
I wish I was never born
So I couldn't make you afraid, my child.
Do you think I am big and strong?
Could I have cried your little tears for you?
Will you believe that I have cried an ocean
As you too must and shall?

Tiger Mountains, Spring 1969

In the Spring of 1969, even the best units we had were suffering. It was hard to look into young faces and not wonder if the country was still worth giving up one's life for. That yes, most Americans in Jackson, Ohio, or Cedar Rapids, Iowa did care, and were proud of us. But we never saw those faces, the faces of the American farmer and worker. All we saw were the traitors leading riots on the campuses. Some of the activists called themselves "Reds," but Reds they were not. Lenin, Mao, and Ho Chi Minh would not have had any use for them. But ruin our morale they did—for that, they were good. Worse still, they found protection under the same laws we were dying for. Some of us never recovered, some of us turned to drugs, while the traitors finished school, became lawyers, businessmen, and media personalities. Today, as I write this, one can see what these traitors have done to our national self-esteem, our morals and ethics, and our economy. They are "CEOs," ride first-class on 747s coast to coast, and drive—you guessed it—not American cars.

Having grown up in a small town, I felt my beliefs secure in the American people and our Constitution. It did not matter to me what Jerry Rubin, Abbie Hoffman, or Jane Fonda said. Fonda, to me, will always be the "Barbarella" we watched under a cargo chute at An Khe. But then, I was twenty-six, and except for the First Sergeant, the guys were eighteen. What would have happened if Betty Grable would have posed on an anti-aircraft gun in Japan?

Reflections During a Monsoon Evening

Some little drops of rain I watch, scooting along the vine
of my lightly strung-out parachute suspension line,
that now supports my tent as shelter from this storm,
from the rain that pours down without recess,
Another stormy day—like so many others,
Rain falls, cold winds blow all through the tropic nights.

I set about my task of boiling water
for my cup of black C-Ration coffee
my solitary evening's repast.
This drop of rain bleeds down so slowly,
on its way to earth's warm embrace.
Should I try to catch it?
My canteen cup will hold another drop—
I'll heat it up for my coffee cup.
Confound it all! Will this rain ever stop?

I am cold and wet, and dream of other places—
Long, cozy evening by some crackling fire.
A big mug of hot tea with a shot of brandy
to warm this place, that feels so cold inside.
Somebody once said;
"Life holds a precious flavor,
the knowledge of which, the protected never find."

I suppose I'll let this drop of rain roll on
Let it go home through the leaves of grass.
But it gives me a sad sentiment,
That all life, like this little drop of rain, must pass.

I too am like that little drop of rain
on my way to some distant hidden stream.
Where I return to, from the place I came
and all this will be no more than just a dream.

The parachute, which so often brought me down
now gives me some shelter from the storm.
Could it be that on some day
my funeral shroud it will become?

Oh yeah though,
Better this, than that which others have,
a man seeks only those he feels his own,
and the guys, those around me now,
are the best companions when that final hour calls.

For this is but a small part of my journey.
Another just like me waited down below.
He cleaned his rifle as he drank his coffee.
Right now he wonders when he'll have to go.

He dreams his idle dreams like I dream mine,
as he plans to put a bullet in my head.
His rifle will with no emotion send
a bullet meant for us and ours to get.
"Forgive, if I do this grave deed to you,
Oh nameless soldier from a distant Land.
I also have a cause to kill you
and abide by orders—like you—
which brought you here to my beloved Land."

I sit and watch the coffee water
stir and gaze at the heating tablet's flame,
and listen to the drops of rain
upon my nylon roof play some sad refrain.

With but half a mind I take my rifle
to check it out, to have another look.
It's clean and ready and feels like ice,
like cold death within my hands.
Cold like a mountain brook.

The magazine is dry with twenty rounds.
If well used it will take some twenty lives.
My hand grenades are untapped and ready;
they too bring death,
they too defuse
a body of some soldier
a body made of flesh like mine.
So many grapes are waiting for harvest.
So many grapes are ripe upon the vine.

But listen well, I'm not complaining.
Sure, I don't like living in this way,
but some men must do our country justice
to keep our way of life as it has been.
There are too many who give only speeches.
Far too many don't even do that.
All they do is live off our great bounty
and complain that they don't have more of that.

There were only a very few
who endured the ice of Valley Forge,
And the folks of the neighboring places
sold food to the Hessians at Trenton
And to the British in their forts.
I'd rather be among the chosen few
who were willing to give life to those sweet sounds
which are engraved upon our Constitution,
engraved on some few hearts when the bugles sound.

Freedom like the glory of the sun
barely shines long on any Land.
Bought not with words, redeemed by red hot blood;
Each generation, one upon another,
this sacred sacrifice must bring!
Hear the sound through my rain-soaked tent.
Above the rain, above the wind,
our Liberty Bell, at home, our freedom's message rings.

It's now, not a question of some right or wrong
now that the die is cast
Nor, who forced the taking up of arms.
The question we are here to answer;
Rests on every heart and mind
"Do we still believe in our future and ourselves,
as those who came before us did
reflected in the precious writing very long ago?"

Do you think there's a better way?
Can you talk the hungry into keeping that sad state?
Men who have nothing give up all they have,
while some of you are going North to cheer the enemy
who kills us.
Is that all you're worth?
If you believe in their way of life
don't preach and sing, but pick a rifle up.
Measure yourself against us here,
as a true believer must.
Share the lives of those you love,
and their fortunes, too.
If you only pay lip service, to both you are untrue.
A traitor of the foulest kind,
with no beliefs to call your own,
like sour grapes unpicked, not to spoil the wine.
A recreant coward is what you are,
No brother at all of mine.

The coffee's hot, not quite; it's barely warm.
So what, I'm far too thirsty
and the raindrop I've been watching is gone,
but will soon return another day.

For you who are all warm and sitting cozy,
whose great worries are sporting games,
will the Browns bomb the Redskins, you ponder
and which victory party to make after the game.

59

To you with the leisure of lovemaking,
What paste to use to make your teeth look white
Or some pill to make your breath smell pleasing
To that male you want to get to bed.

To all you guys who just love your fun and games,
whose only claim to manhood is a cheer,
who elaborate their greater manly glory
at the postgame bash over booze and beer.
I think under this nylon canopy
and laugh an empty laugh at all you clowns.
Most all the brave youth of our country are not at home…
they're sitting around me now.
To those who did their share, we greet you.
You deserve your comfort and your rest.
You are those whose footsteps we are tracing
whose example now our manhood tests.
To all the farmers and fieldhands behind the plow
who work from early morning until late into the night,
To the worker with his dirty hands, our greetings!
Your efforts make our country the best.

The briefest moments like this rainy day
are broken by the thunder of the shell.
The blast of some exploding mortar
echoes through the valley of the deadly,
echoes through the valley of the Anh Loa
and is about to send someone to hell.
The sound sweeps past, and rolling past my tent does ask—
"Will this rain ever stop? Will this rain ever stop?
Could it be that this very rainy day will be my very Last?"
Will my belly filled with lukewarm coffee keep its liquid,
or will some fiery blast, tear it open and let it spill
mingled with my blood upon the ground?
My streaming intestines cover this Palmetto covered mound of
earth where my parachute tent soaked with water stands to
await the coming of the night.

60

Oh God, what are you doing now?
My love is so far away.
There's been not one letter from you
since I went away.
It's been so long—six months today—
all have written except you.
I'm so worried; perhaps you're sick.
Perhaps I'm losing you.
How many cold and rainy nights I close my eyes to see
Only your beloved face—how you are killing me!

Above the monsoon clouds I hear the thunder of a bomber.
I bet that guy up there is dry.
Not that his lot is easier than mine
but I sure would like to trade his place for this of mine.
The sound of shells exploding now is joined by machine gun
fire.
Time for my companions and I to pack and be moving on.
The guy who is out looking for us must have had his coffee
early.
I think we'll show up where he does
but we'll be there before he will.
After awhile, the world will be still,
and dark night will come upon the Land.
To some dark death—
To those of us alive,
Darkness of another sleepless rainy monsoon night.

Summer 1969

The world is bathed in soft, bright fluorescent-like moonlight almost bright enough to read by, but not quite. The shadows of the coconut palm forest are dark, and make the shafts of moonlight that penetrate like pillars of silver. There is a lukewarm breeze blowing from the South China Sea just over the mountain. It keeps the mosquitoes down. The combat patrol of American paratroopers moves noiselessly in the shadows as though on cushions of air. The point man stops, lifts his hand, and the young squad leader moves up beside him.

A tiny little village, peaceful in slumber, fills the view within a clearing. The silence is heavy, broken by the grunting of a few hogs, and the scented summer air smells of a mixture of charcoal, incense, and nuoc mam (fish sauce). There is a little well with some baskets and earthen jars around it near a wall of bamboo. The bamboo encloses one side of the settlement and gives protection from the prevailing winds that lash the land during the monsoon season. The patrol leader signals only with his hands. The squad moves noiselessly, clinging to the shadows.

Suddenly, the night is broken by the cry of a little baby startled in its sleep. A moment later, a man in black pajama pants jumps through an open window and runs like hell down the street. The point man and the grenadier next to the squad leader are about to fire, but the leader motions them not to. The young man disappears behind the bamboo, and only a little dust cloud on the village street hints that he had been there. The child's sobs are a little muffled. I can imagine a mother, desperately afraid, covering its mouth and waiting for the sound of gunfire, the detonation of grenades, and the fire that will destroy her village and home. Death is near, but there is silence. She begins to nurse her child to keep it quiet. What was it? Were they the dreaded Americans with their unpredictable kindness, or the feared North Vietnamese sappers with their righteous and cruel political cadremen who spoke with a funny accent and always wanted food? It wasn't the local Viet Cong platoon. They were all dead now. It didn't really matter. All that was important was the village, the family, and getting enough food to eat. One wife this night was not a widow come morning, nor was her child an orphan.

My Child

Sleep, my child; sleep.
They're gone away.
So sleep, my child;
Don't cry.
They have passed this way,
But briefly,
And now they have left
And gone their way.

Sleep, my child; sleep.
There is no need to weep.
They are on their way
To distant places.
Soon you won't recall their faces.
So go to sleep, my child;
Don't cry.
They had to go and went away.

Don't cry; just sleep, my child,
For soon the sun will rise again,
And you will laugh, not cry;
So sleep. They have gone away;
For them,
There is no other way.
The soldiers—they have gone away.
Only graves will mark their stay.

Back Home

I was sitting alone, as usual, on the floor of my living room at Fort Bragg, North Carolina. I was about to have supper and turned on the television to watch the evening news. President Nixon announced the cease-fire in Vietnam. I cried long and hard. It was not the cease-fire that made me cry, but the many things it brought to mind. I remembered the many friends who never came home, and those who did come home that were unable to deal with life now. I recalled how some years before, on my way to Australia on Rest and Recreation, the captain of the 707 woke us up some place over New Guinea and announced that we had a new president, Richard M. Nixon. The plane was full of troops, and they virtually went wild. Now we had a president who would bring us home with a semblance of honor—that's all we wanted. Honor was very important to the American soldier. We felt it was the least we could ask for, since the country wouldn't allow us to win. Now the President, on whom we pinned our hopes, had let us down by agreeing to a cease-fire instead of pressing on to victory.

The Ghosts

When the sun sets and mountains cast black shadows,
Countless ghosts march through bloody, smoke-filled meadows.
There are no bands and no cheering crowds,
Only the sounds of empty canisters, the clicks of
soundless rounds.
When the steam of Mother Earth's body,
Rises up from the paddy fields below,
You see with sightless eyes…
Our ghosts marching in the fading glow.
There are no bugles; there are no medals here.
For only those alive wear graveyards on their chests
Their greatest deed, perhaps, was to put us to our rest.
No, ghosts don't care for marching bands and such;
Nor care they for the praise of laughing, cheering crowds.
Only now and then they wish that they could cry…
but ghosts cannot.

A rusty helmet in the grass abandoned,
Plays their tattoo when tropic raindrops fall,
And blackened ruins of some nameless village
Are for their kind our famed renowned halls.
Nor do they cradle their children in their arms,
Or kiss their wives and loves a fond hello,
For long forgotten…they are kissed by others now!
Yes, ghosts do march, and ghostly children follow—
Little boys and girls who died with them—
No kin in flesh, but one in death and sorrow.

The endless lines of ghostly grenadiers,
And soldiers who went far away to war,
Now by the grieving, speechless moon,
Greet their former enemies and are brothers here once more.
But even ghostly armies have their feelings,
For some are only half or partly dead;

They ask of those alive, "What's all this cheering?
Can this be the reason why we all have bled?"
Our colors, our proud standard,
Our dear flag was taken home—away from where we fell.
No honor, no monument marks the place of hell.
Our bodies, too they've taken home, but our ghosts must stay;
Our wandering in the paddy fields starts at the end of day.
Sightless eyes search through the night
For a sign that we have conquered
Right or wrong, it was our fight!
Right or wrong, we died for right!

The wind a marching song does play
Through the bullet holes of a helmet
The infantry, the Legionnaires are marching in review,
but their officers are young and few.
The Chaplain with his sightless eyes the Holy Mass does say
Upon an altar of palm logs festooned with blood and clay.
At the Mass they are all praying…ghosts cannot decay—
They only feel deep sorrow because their leaders went away.
There are no smiling faces here, just sightless, glassy eyes
Who never saw their loves again, for whom now no one cries.
"Oh grief, oh grief; was it all in vain? Is this for what we
died?"
Even the price of victory in death was us denied.